This Guest book CELEBRATES

_____'S

30TH BIRTHDAY

THE BIRTHDAY GUEST BOOK

GUEST NAME(S)   MESSAGE & *BEST WISHES*

ADDRESS /
TELEPOHONE /
EMAIL

THE BIRTHDAY GUEST BOOK

GUEST NAME(S)   **MESSAGE & *BEST WISHES***

ADDRESS / TELEPOHONE / EMAIL

THE BIRTHDAY GUEST BOOK

GUEST NAME(S) **MESSAGE & *BEST WISHES***

ADDRESS / TELEPOHONE / EMAIL

THE BIRTHDAY GUEST BOOK

GUEST NAME(S) MESSAGE & *BEST WISHES*

ADDRESS /
TELEPOHONE /
EMAIL

THE BIRTHDAY GUEST BOOK

GUEST NAME(S)   MESSAGE & *BEST WISHES*

ADDRESS /
TELEPOHONE /
EMAIL

THE BIRTHDAY GUEST BOOK

GUEST NAME(S)   *MESSAGE & BEST WISHES*

ADDRESS / TELEPOHONE / EMAIL

THE BIRTHDAY GUEST BOOK

GUEST NAME(S)   MESSAGE & *BEST WISHES*

ADDRESS / *TELEPOHONE* / *EMAIL*

THE BIRTHDAY GUEST BOOK

GUEST NAME(S) **MESSAGE & *BEST WISHES***

**ADDRESS /
TELEPOHONE /
EMAIL**

THE BIRTHDAY GUEST BOOK

GUEST NAME(S)   MESSAGE & *BEST WISHES*

ADDRESS /
TELEPOHONE /
EMAIL

THE BIRTHDAY GUEST BOOK

GUEST NAME(S) **MESSAGE & *BEST WISHES***

*ADDRESS /
TELEPOHONE /
EMAIL*

THE BIRTHDAY GUEST BOOK

GUEST NAME(S)   MESSAGE & *BEST WISHES*

ADDRESS /
TELEPOHONE /
EMAIL

THE BIRTHDAY GUEST BOOK

GUEST NAME(S) **MESSAGE & *BEST WISHES***

ADDRESS / TELEPOHONE / EMAIL

THE BIRTHDAY GUEST BOOK

GUEST NAME(S)

MESSAGE & *BEST WISHES*

**ADDRESS /
TELEPOHONE /
EMAIL**

THE BIRTHDAY GUEST BOOK

GUEST NAME(S) **MESSAGE & *BEST WISHES***

**ADDRESS /
TELEPOHONE /
EMAIL**

THE BIRTHDAY GUEST BOOK

GUEST NAME(S)   MESSAGE & *BEST WISHES*

ADDRESS /
TELEPOHONE /
EMAIL

THE BIRTHDAY GUEST BOOK

GUEST NAME(S)　　　MESSAGE & *BEST WISHES*

ADDRESS /
TELEPOHONE /
EMAIL

THE BIRTHDAY GUEST BOOK

GUEST NAME(S)

MESSAGE & *BEST WISHES*

ADDRESS /
TELEPOHONE /
EMAIL

THE BIRTHDAY GUEST BOOK

GUEST NAME(S) MESSAGE & *BEST WISHES*

ADDRESS /
TELEPOHONE /
EMAIL

THE BIRTHDAY GUEST BOOK

GUEST NAME(S)   **MESSAGE & *BEST WISHES***

ADDRESS / TELEPOHONE / EMAIL

THE BIRTHDAY GUEST BOOK

GUEST NAME(S) **MESSAGE & *BEST WISHES***

**ADDRESS /
TELEPOHONE /
EMAIL**

THE BIRTHDAY GUEST BOOK

GUEST NAME(S)　　　MESSAGE & *BEST WISHES*

ADDRESS /
TELEPOHONE /
EMAIL

THE BIRTHDAY GUEST BOOK

GUEST NAME(S)

MESSAGE & *BEST WISHES*

ADDRESS /
TELEPOHONE /
EMAIL

THE BIRTHDAY GUEST BOOK

GUEST NAME(S) MESSAGE & *BEST WISHES*

ADDRESS /
TELEPOHONE /
EMAIL

THE BIRTHDAY GUEST BOOK

GUEST NAME(S) **MESSAGE & *BEST WISHES***

**ADDRESS /
TELEPOHONE /
EMAIL**

THE BIRTHDAY GUEST BOOK

GUEST NAME(S)　　　　　MESSAGE & *BEST WISHES*

ADDRESS /
TELEPOHONE /
EMAIL

THE BIRTHDAY GUEST BOOK

GUEST NAME(S)

MESSAGE & *BEST WISHES*

ADDRESS /
TELEPOHONE /
EMAIL

THE BIRTHDAY GUEST BOOK

GUEST NAME(S)   MESSAGE & *BEST WISHES*

ADDRESS / TELEPOHONE / EMAIL

THE BIRTHDAY GUEST BOOK

GUEST NAME(S) **MESSAGE & *BEST WISHES***

**ADDRESS /
TELEPOHONE /
EMAIL**

THE BIRTHDAY GUEST BOOK

GUEST NAME(S)　　　　MESSAGE & *BEST WISHES*

ADDRESS /
TELEPOHONE /
EMAIL

THE BIRTHDAY GUEST BOOK

GUEST NAME(S)

MESSAGE & *BEST WISHES*

ADDRESS /
TELEPOHONE /
EMAIL

THE BIRTHDAY GUEST BOOK

GUEST NAME(S)

MESSAGE & *BEST WISHES*

ADDRESS /
TELEPOHONE /
EMAIL

THE BIRTHDAY GUEST BOOK

GUEST NAME(S) **MESSAGE & *BEST WISHES***

ADDRESS / TELEPOHONE / EMAIL

THE BIRTHDAY GUEST BOOK

GUEST NAME(S) MESSAGE & *BEST WISHES*

ADDRESS /
TELEPOHONE /
EMAIL

THE BIRTHDAY GUEST BOOK

GUEST NAME(S)

MESSAGE & *BEST WISHES*

ADDRESS /
TELEPOHONE /
EMAIL

THE BIRTHDAY GUEST BOOK

GUEST NAME(S)

MESSAGE & *BEST WISHES*

ADDRESS /
TELEPOHONE /
EMAIL

THE BIRTHDAY GUEST BOOK

GUEST NAME(S)   MESSAGE & *BEST WISHES*

ADDRESS /
TELEPOHONE /
EMAIL

THE BIRTHDAY GUEST BOOK

GUEST NAME(S)   MESSAGE & *BEST WISHES*

ADDRESS /
TELEPOHONE /
EMAIL

THE BIRTHDAY GUEST BOOK

GUEST NAME(S)   MESSAGE & *BEST WISHES*

ADDRESS /
TELEPOHONE /
EMAIL

THE BIRTHDAY GUEST BOOK

GUEST NAME(S)   **MESSAGE & *BEST WISHES***

ADDRESS / TELEPOHONE / EMAIL

THE BIRTHDAY GUEST BOOK

GUEST NAME(S) MESSAGE & *BEST WISHES*

ADDRESS /
TELEPOHONE /
EMAIL

THE BIRTHDAY GUEST BOOK

GUEST NAME(S) **MESSAGE & *BEST WISHES***

*ADDRESS /
TELEPOHONE /
EMAIL*

THE BIRTHDAY GUEST BOOK

GUEST NAME(S) **MESSAGE & *BEST WISHES***

ADDRESS / TELEPOHONE / EMAIL

THE BIRTHDAY GUEST BOOK

GUEST NAME(S) MESSAGE & *BEST WISHES*

ADDRESS / TELEPOHONE / EMAIL

THE BIRTHDAY GUEST BOOK

GUEST NAME(S) MESSAGE & *BEST WISHES*

ADDRESS /
TELEPOHONE /
EMAIL

THE BIRTHDAY GUEST BOOK

GUEST NAME(S)　　　MESSAGE & *BEST WISHES*

ADDRESS /
TELEPOHONE /
EMAIL

THE BIRTHDAY GUEST BOOK

GUEST NAME(S) MESSAGE & *BEST WISHES*

ADDRESS /
TELEPOHONE /
EMAIL

THE BIRTHDAY GUEST BOOK

GUEST NAME(S) **MESSAGE & *BEST WISHES***

ADDRESS / TELEPOHONE / EMAIL

THE BIRTHDAY GUEST BOOK

GUEST NAME(S) **MESSAGE & *BEST WISHES***

ADDRESS / TELEPOHONE / EMAIL

THE BIRTHDAY GUEST BOOK

GUEST NAME(S)　　MESSAGE & *BEST WISHES*

ADDRESS /
*TELEPOHONE /
EMAIL*

THE BIRTHDAY GUEST BOOK

GUEST NAME(S)

MESSAGE & *BEST WISHES*

ADDRESS /
TELEPOHONE /
EMAIL

THE BIRTHDAY GUEST BOOK

GUEST NAME(S) MESSAGE & *BEST WISHES*

ADDRESS /
TELEPOHONE /
EMAIL

THE BIRTHDAY GUEST BOOK

GUEST NAME(S)   MESSAGE & *BEST WISHES*

ADDRESS /
TELEPOHONE /
EMAIL

THE BIRTHDAY GUEST BOOK

GUEST NAME(S)   MESSAGE & *BEST WISHES*

ADDRESS /
TELEPOHONE /
EMAIL

THE BIRTHDAY GUEST BOOK

GUEST NAME(S)   *MESSAGE & BEST WISHES*

**ADDRESS /
TELEPOHONE /
EMAIL**

THE BIRTHDAY GUEST BOOK

GUEST NAME(S)

MESSAGE & *BEST WISHES*

ADDRESS / TELEPOHONE / EMAIL

THE BIRTHDAY GUEST BOOK

GUEST NAME(S)

MESSAGE & *BEST WISHES*

ADDRESS /
TELEPOHONE /
EMAIL

THE BIRTHDAY GUEST BOOK

GUEST NAME(S)   **MESSAGE & *BEST WISHES***

*ADDRESS /
TELEPOHONE /
EMAIL*

THE BIRTHDAY GUEST BOOK

GUEST NAME(S)   **MESSAGE & *BEST WISHES***

*ADDRESS /
TELEPOHONE /
EMAIL*

THE BIRTHDAY GUEST BOOK

GUEST NAME(S)   MESSAGE & *BEST WISHES*

ADDRESS /
TELEPOHONE /
EMAIL

THE BIRTHDAY GUEST BOOK

GUEST NAME(S)

MESSAGE & *BEST WISHES*

ADDRESS /
TELEPOHONE /
EMAIL

THE BIRTHDAY GUEST BOOK

GUEST NAME(S)　　　MESSAGE & *BEST WISHES*

ADDRESS /
TELEPOHONE /
EMAIL

THE BIRTHDAY GUEST BOOK

GUEST NAME(S)　　　MESSAGE & *BEST WISHES*

ADDRESS /
TELEPOHONE /
EMAIL

THE BIRTHDAY GUEST BOOK

GUEST NAME(S)   **MESSAGE & *BEST WISHES***

ADDRESS /
TELEPOHONE /
EMAIL

THE BIRTHDAY GUEST BOOK

GUEST NAME(S) **MESSAGE & *BEST WISHES***

ADDRESS / TELEPOHONE / EMAIL

THE BIRTHDAY GUEST BOOK

GUEST NAME(S) **MESSAGE & *BEST WISHES***

**ADDRESS /
TELEPOHONE /
EMAIL**

THE BIRTHDAY GUEST BOOK

GUEST NAME(S) *MESSAGE & BEST WISHES*

**ADDRESS /
TELEPOHONE /
EMAIL**

THE BIRTHDAY GUEST BOOK

GUEST NAME(S)   **MESSAGE & *BEST WISHES***

ADDRESS /
TELEPOHONE /
EMAIL

THE BIRTHDAY GUEST BOOK

GUEST NAME(S)   MESSAGE & *BEST WISHES*

ADDRESS / TELEPOHONE / EMAIL

THE BIRTHDAY GUEST BOOK

GUEST NAME(S) **MESSAGE & *BEST WISHES***

ADDRESS / TELEPOHONE / EMAIL

THE BIRTHDAY GUEST BOOK

GUEST NAME(S)   MESSAGE & *BEST WISHES*

ADDRESS /
TELEPOHONE /
EMAIL

THE BIRTHDAY GUEST BOOK

GUEST NAME(S)   **MESSAGE & *BEST WISHES***

ADDRESS / TELEPOHONE / EMAIL

THE BIRTHDAY GUEST BOOK

GUEST NAME(S)   MESSAGE & *BEST WISHES*

ADDRESS /
TELEPOHONE /
EMAIL

THE BIRTHDAY GUEST BOOK

GUEST NAME(S)   MESSAGE & *BEST WISHES*

ADDRESS /
TELEPOHONE /
EMAIL

THE BIRTHDAY GUEST BOOK

GUEST NAME(S) MESSAGE & *BEST WISHES*

ADDRESS /
TELEPOHONE /
EMAIL

THE BIRTHDAY GUEST BOOK

GUEST NAME(S)   MESSAGE & *BEST WISHES*

ADDRESS /
TELEPOHONE /
EMAIL

THE BIRTHDAY GUEST BOOK

GUEST NAME(S)　　　MESSAGE & *BEST WISHES*

ADDRESS /
TELEPOHONE /
EMAIL

THE BIRTHDAY GUEST BOOK

GUEST NAME(S)

MESSAGE & BEST WISHES

ADDRESS /
TELEPOHONE /
EMAIL

THE BIRTHDAY GUEST BOOK

GUEST NAME(S) **MESSAGE & *BEST WISHES***

ADDRESS / TELEPOHONE / EMAIL

THE BIRTHDAY GUEST BOOK

GUEST NAME(S) MESSAGE & *BEST WISHES*

ADDRESS /
TELEPOHONE /
EMAIL

THE BIRTHDAY GUEST BOOK

GUEST NAME(S)   **MESSAGE & *BEST WISHES***

**ADDRESS /
TELEPOHONE /
EMAIL**

THE BIRTHDAY GUEST BOOK

GUEST NAME(S)   MESSAGE & *BEST WISHES*

ADDRESS /
TELEPOHONE /
EMAIL

THE BIRTHDAY GUEST BOOK

GUEST NAME(S)   MESSAGE & *BEST WISHES*

ADDRESS /
TELEPOHONE /
EMAIL

THE BIRTHDAY GUEST BOOK

GUEST NAME(S)

MESSAGE & *BEST WISHES*

ADDRESS /
TELEPOHONE /
EMAIL

THE BIRTHDAY GUEST BOOK

GUEST NAME(S) **MESSAGE & *BEST WISHES***

ADDRESS / TELEPOHONE / EMAIL

THE BIRTHDAY GUEST BOOK

GUEST NAME(S)

MESSAGE & *BEST WISHES*

ADDRESS /
*TELEPOHONE /
EMAIL*

THE BIRTHDAY GUEST BOOK

GUEST NAME(S)

MESSAGE & *BEST WISHES*

ADDRESS /
TELEPOHONE /
EMAIL

THE BIRTHDAY GUEST BOOK

GUEST NAME(S)   MESSAGE & *BEST WISHES*

ADDRESS /
TELEPOHONE /
EMAIL

THE BIRTHDAY GUEST BOOK

GUEST NAME(S) **MESSAGE & *BEST WISHES***

**ADDRESS /
TELEPOHONE /
EMAIL**

THE BIRTHDAY GUEST BOOK

GUEST NAME(S) MESSAGE & *BEST WISHES*

ADDRESS / TELEPOHONE / EMAIL

THE BIRTHDAY GUEST BOOK

GUEST NAME(S)　　　MESSAGE & *BEST WISHES*

*ADDRESS /
TELEPOHONE /
EMAIL*

THE BIRTHDAY GUEST BOOK

GUEST NAME(S)   MESSAGE & *BEST WISHES*

ADDRESS /
TELEPOHONE /
EMAIL

THE BIRTHDAY GUEST BOOK

GUEST NAME(S) **MESSAGE & *BEST WISHES***

ADDRESS / TELEPOHONE / EMAIL

THE BIRTHDAY GUEST BOOK

GUEST NAME(S)   MESSAGE & *BEST WISHES*

ADDRESS /
TELEPOHONE /
EMAIL

THE BIRTHDAY GUEST BOOK

GUEST NAME(S) MESSAGE & *BEST WISHES*

ADDRESS /
TELEPOHONE /
EMAIL

THE BIRTHDAY GUEST BOOK

GUEST NAME(S)   **MESSAGE & *BEST WISHES***

ADDRESS / TELEPOHONE / EMAIL

THE BIRTHDAY GUEST BOOK

GUEST NAME(S)   **MESSAGE & *BEST WISHES***

**ADDRESS /
TELEPOHONE /
EMAIL**

THE BIRTHDAY GUEST BOOK

GUEST NAME(S)   MESSAGE & *BEST WISHES*

ADDRESS /
TELEPOHONE /
EMAIL

THE BIRTHDAY GUEST BOOK

GUEST NAME(S)   MESSAGE & *BEST WISHES*

ADDRESS /
TELEPOHONE /
EMAIL

THE BIRTHDAY GUEST BOOK

GUEST NAME(S)   MESSAGE & *BEST WISHES*

ADDRESS /
TELEPOHONE /
EMAIL

THE BIRTHDAY GUEST BOOK

GUEST NAME(S) MESSAGE & *BEST WISHES*

ADDRESS /
TELEPOHONE /
EMAIL

THE BIRTHDAY GUEST BOOK

GUEST NAME(S)　　　　MESSAGE & *BEST WISHES*

ADDRESS /
TELEPOHONE /
EMAIL

THE BIRTHDAY GUEST BOOK

GUEST NAME(S)　　　MESSAGE & *BEST WISHES*

ADDRESS /
TELEPOHONE /
EMAIL

THE BIRTHDAY GUEST BOOK

GUEST NAME(S)   MESSAGE & *BEST WISHES*

ADDRESS /
TELEPOHONE /
EMAIL

THE BIRTHDAY GUEST BOOK

GUEST NAME(S)   MESSAGE & *BEST WISHES*

ADDRESS /
*TELEPOHONE /
EMAIL*

THE BIRTHDAY GUEST BOOK

GUEST NAME(S) **MESSAGE & *BEST WISHES***

*ADDRESS /
TELEPOHONE /
EMAIL*

THE BIRTHDAY GUEST BOOK

GUEST NAME(S)   **MESSAGE & *BEST WISHES***

*ADDRESS /
TELEPOHONE /
EMAIL*

THE BIRTHDAY GUEST BOOK

GUEST NAME(S) MESSAGE & *BEST WISHES*

ADDRESS /
TELEPOHONE /
EMAIL

THE BIRTHDAY GUEST BOOK

GUEST NAME(S)   **MESSAGE & *BEST WISHES***

**ADDRESS /
TELEPOHONE /
EMAIL**

THE BIRTHDAY GUEST BOOK

GUEST NAME(S) *MESSAGE & BEST WISHES*

**ADDRESS /
TELEPOHONE /
EMAIL**

THE BIRTHDAY GUEST BOOK

GUEST NAME(S) MESSAGE & *BEST WISHES*

ADDRESS /
TELEPOHONE /
EMAIL

THE BIRTHDAY GUEST BOOK

GUEST NAME(S)

MESSAGE & *BEST WISHES*

ADDRESS /
TELEPOHONE /
EMAIL

THE BIRTHDAY GUEST BOOK

GUEST NAME(S)

MESSAGE & *BEST WISHES*

ADDRESS /
TELEPOHONE /
EMAIL

THE BIRTHDAY GUEST BOOK

GUEST NAME(S) **MESSAGE & *BEST WISHES***

**ADDRESS /
TELEPOHONE /
EMAIL**

THE BIRTHDAY GUEST BOOK

GUEST NAME(S) MESSAGE & *BEST WISHES*

ADDRESS / TELEPOHONE / EMAIL

THE BIRTHDAY GUEST BOOK

GUEST NAME(S)　　　　MESSAGE & *BEST WISHES*

ADDRESS /
TELEPOHONE /
EMAIL

THE BIRTHDAY GUEST BOOK

GUEST NAME(S) **MESSAGE & *BEST WISHES***

ADDRESS / TELEPOHONE / EMAIL

THE BIRTHDAY GUEST BOOK

GUEST NAME(S)　　　　MESSAGE & BEST WISHES

ADDRESS /
TELEPOHONE /
EMAIL

THE BIRTHDAY GUEST BOOK

GUEST NAME(S)　　　MESSAGE & *BEST WISHES*

ADDRESS /
TELEPOHONE /
EMAIL

THE BIRTHDAY GUEST BOOK

GUEST NAME(S) MESSAGE & *BEST WISHES*

ADDRESS /
TELEPOHONE /
EMAIL

Made in United States
Troutdale, OR
01/11/2025